A FRIEND THAT I CAN DO FOR

A FRIEND THAT I CAN DO FOR

Stories from Ravenswood Community Services at All Saints' Episcopal Church

Interviews by Anne Ford

Photographs by Charlie Simokaitis

Design by Allison Schloss and Madison Berry

This book is for the hungry.
May we all be fed.

Listen! I am standing at the door, knocking; if you hear my voice and open the door, I will come in to you and eat with you, and you with me.

Revelation 3:20

PREFACE

Nearly every Tuesday night for 20 years and counting, scores of hungry people have showed up at All Saints' Episcopal Church in Chicago's Ravenswood neighborhood. They're there for a bag of groceries and a hot, family-style dinner, both made available through Ravenswood Community Services.

Some get their food and go. Others—many others—make an evening of it. They joke and chat with each other in line, ask what's being served that night, and see each other safely to the bus or el stop afterward. Or they sit quietly at a table, not saying much at all, but clearly enjoying the chatter and company.

At the beginning of my stint as an RCS volunteer, I thought I'd be setting tables or washing dishes (two very important tasks when more than 100 people are coming to dinner!). But the biggest need, I was told, was for volunteers to simply hang out and talk with those who came to dine.

As I learned, many people who are hungry for food are equally hungry for conversation, even small talk of the "How 'bout that weather?" kind. Many, too, are hungry to be of service to others. One regular I got to know insisted on pulling out chairs and getting cups of water for those who shared his table. As he told me (in the phrase that lent its title to this book): "I have to have a friend that I can do for."

After a while, I too found myself hungry for a deeper connection. I looked at volunteers and guests alike and thought: Who were these people when they weren't with us? What were their hopes and fears and histories? And would they tell me if I asked?

They would. They did. Here we are. Please: Dig in.

— Anne Ford
September 2013

CONTENTS

BEAU 22
"I said, 'I really have no idea what I'm doing, but yes.'"

CASEY 23
"Ninety percent of my friends are gay, lesbian, bi, something."

"LARRY"* 25
"You never want to tangle with a Free Methodist."

FRAN 28
"I finally decided: I have got to follow this."

"DONNA"* 31
"I'm very comfortable around people that might be messy, including myself."

JOE 33
"Three years later, here I am."

BONNIE 35

GALE 36

MARY 38
"The more I go, the deeper it gets."

MIKE 40
"I always stay working, no matter what."

ROB 42
"I walked out of there with something the kids on the Gold Coast would wear."

JULIE 46
  "If I drop over dead and nothing happens, big deal."

SYLVESTER 50
  "I see people just staring at their cell phone. I don't get it."

SAM 54
  "My days of being kicked in the head for a living are pretty much over."

LORI 56
  "I was a fast worker, thank God."

MICHAEL 60
  "Okay, so two percent. That's not going to happen, right?"

"ANDY"* 62
  "I can take something from nothing and make a meal of it."

LORI G. 65

LORRAINE 66

"GLORIA"* 67
  "He turned around to see me—then he was smiling a lot more."

"LUIS"* 69
  "I need the company of people, you know? But good people."

*Name changed

Andrea

ANDREA

The first day I volunteered, it was really, really awkward. I thought I was supposed to talk to people and entertain them, but they talked to each other. I'd go sit down at a table and eat and they'd look at me like, "What are you doing? Why are you sitting here with us?" I clearly wasn't sitting down at dinner because I needed to.

Eventually I got to know some people and became friends. If you sit down and eat with someone week after week after week, something happens between you. Sometimes they tell me about their lives, and sometimes I tell them about my life. If I'm asking them to tell me about their lives, who am I to think I can't return that?

My father has stomach cancer. Food pantry was the day after I got the news, and one of them said to me, "Are you tired? What's wrong?"

I said, "My father called me last night to say he has cancer."

He said, "Well, I'll pray for you."

I said, "Would you pray for my dad, too?"

He said, "Yeah. Better yet, let's pray together."

I was just like, *Oh, shit.*

I said, "Okay, that would be nice."

He took my hands in his, and he started saying the Lord's

Prayer. He doesn't remember my name. He calls me Purty. So he said, "God, please take care of Purty's dad." I was bawling. There's not very many people I pray with. You know? Especially out loud.

It's one of the highlights of my week. It doesn't make me sad. It's sort of a social occasion. I see my friends, and I hang out for a couple hours and have a meal. How often do you get to have a dinner party with your friends every week? Where you don't have to cook and you don't have to clean up? If I were a good volunteer, I would clean up.

The folks on Sunday morning, we look like we have our lives together. We can hide all of the things that are falling apart. Most of the folks on Tuesday night can't hide the fact that their lives are falling apart. They're much more forgiving. If you say something stupid or don't respond right, they don't judge. You're one of them.

People are lonely. People are really, really lonely.

"LUKE"

I was born and raised on the North Side. The way they talk on the South Side, they don't understand me, and I don't understand slang. I don't go out there no more. They are scandalous. Everybody done turned scandalous.

Around the time I got born, they threw my dad on a mental ward. When I got about 10 years old, they let him out of the hospital. My mom tells me, "Go help your dad out the cab." First time I ever seen my dad. I opened the door, and I helped him to the house, and everything was okay.

I got introduced to drugs at a very young age. By the time I was 13, I was in Reed Mental Health Center. I just kept getting high. My counselor, we were getting high together in his office. When I was 16, they let me go to high school. I had a girlfriend, and she did my work. All I did was play sports. That's why I can't read and write nothing.

I left home because these gangbangers kept fronting me drugs. It brings too much drama. About three months later, my truck died on me right outside of Illinois Masonic Hospital. I called my mom: "Mom, I need a new motor." My mom tells me there's nothing she can do for me. I said, "Oh, no," and I started crying. I'm trying to figure out what am I gonna do. It's snowing.

It dawned on me: just go back to the projects where I was born and raised, and stay in the hallway. That's what I did. Then the gangbangers ran me out. So I went to Damen Bridge, and I was all right. They built it where you can go under the bridge. That's where I was sleeping for 10 years.

The last job I had, I was working out of the YMCA that I live at. But I stopped doing that because I'm not ready to have all this extra money. I have to have a friend that I can do *for*. If I'm by myself, depression will set in. If I got, let's say, $800 in my pocket, and I can't find anybody to take out to dinner, or do anything that normal people do, the devil gets into my mind, and I'm doing the wrong thing. I don't want the money, because I know what I'm capable of doing, and I just don't want to do that.

I was house-sitting for a guy who had to go to prison for two months. He came and dug me up from under the bridge to sit with this 80-year-old lady till he gets back. The lady, if she put anything on the stove to cook, she'd walk off and forget about it. I told her, "Don't cook nothing. I will cook for you."

I had money, so I went to Aldi's. I cooked a duck. I had it on the table. I had candles lit. I ran to the liquor store and bought some Boone Farm Strawberry Hill. She tastes it—I made her a plate and everything—and she tells me in her 80 years of life, ain't no man in her life ever did what I just did. I said, "Oh, my Lord." What's wrong with these people that this lady's dealing with?

STEVE

I'm from Missouri. I've got two kids there, and my mother and my sister help take care of 'em for me so I'm able to stay here and work. I get to go home once a year.

If I didn't have my kids, my life would be a lot different. Back then I really didn't give a damn about anything. But when my girls were born, it straightened me up quickly. Especially once they started to talk. It makes you feel so good inside. How could you hurt something like that?

I made a promise to my mom that every week I'd send $200 home. Sometimes if I run a little short, my ma'll write me a letter and throw a few dollars in an envelope and tell me it's from the girls.

You gotta be a positive-thinking person in this world nowadays. If you're a negative-thinking person, you're going down the drain. I always try to be jolly-go-lucky. Always. Your feelings can make you, and they can break you. As long as my family's taken care of and I got me a nice warm place to go, I got me a good hot meal a day in my stomach, I'm cool.

I do a lot of talking to myself when I'm walking. I found that's the best time to talk to Jesus. If I know I'm about ready to do something wrong, I ask, "What do you think I should do?" He tells you, "That's up to you." He's gotten me out of a lot of trouble and kept me out of a lot of trouble. But no matter how powerful he is, he can't be with you 24/7, because if he were, we wouldn't make mistakes, would we?

Karen

Stephanie

Annie and Gabriella

ANNIE

My parents left their home in the suburbs as soon as they found out they were pregnant with me, because they wanted to raise me in the city. This was just a couple years after Martin Luther King was saying that Chicagoans ought to integrate their neighborhoods. I've had people ask me, "Are your parents hippies?" and the answer is, "No, my parents are Christians."

At the hospital where I'm a nurse, they say I work so well with all of my black patients and black families. We're talking *deep* South Side. But wealthy white people scare me.

My patient from last night was a healthy girl who had a brain bleed and is now completely brain-damaged. The child who comes in for an appendectomy and goes home—I care about him for four days and then he's gone. It's the recurrent kids—"Oh, Joshua's back!"—that wind up being my obsessive conversation.

When I first started coming to church here, I had finished college and was living in a little apartment a couple blocks away. I was trying to make friends, so I went to a vegetarian commune that had once-a-week potlucks. I did that for almost a year, and one day I came in and I looked around, and not a single person there knew my name. We just talked about "free Tibet" or whatever.

I came to All Saints, and everybody remembered me and asked me how I was doing. It was not: "I'm coming here to donate my time for those poor people." It was: "I've been living here in Chicago and riding the train to work and paying my bills and it's been the most isolating, cold experience. This is the first time all week that somebody's looked me in the eye." Don't ever be 22. It is miserable.

I used to do the grocery bags. I cook when they need cooks. I try to go upstairs and just hang out with folks. I'm so not-gregarious that I have a tendency not to hold up my half of the conversation, which is fine, because a lot of the people at Tuesday night food pantry are people who will hold up two halves of a conversation. All you have to do is smile and nod, which is so easy and so restful.

I started thinking about adopting in fourth grade, because my Cabbage Patch Kid was adopted. By the time I was in high school, I realized I had no intention of having children through marriage. At this point, I'm as stable as I'm going to be. I have an income, I have a home, I have a support network. Be ready to be supportive! You have to show up with a casserole, because you're Episcopalian!

I looked into all of the different options, and I decided to try my luck with DCFS. I said, "I'm open to any race." The social worker asked me 100 questions about race: "What will you do with her hair? What will you say when she's in kindergarten?" She was not going to give me a black child unless I could pass every test. Because there have been problems in the past with people who are like, 'Well, I saw a black person on the *Cosby Show*.'"

JOSEPH

What is different is how each person ends up homeless. Once you end up homeless, a lot of the story becomes the same.

I was a truck driver. I got divorced, and rather than stay and kill her, it was easier to leave and let her live. It's been going on nine years now.

I ended up at a shelter. You had to get in this line. You had to strip down and take a shower. You had to wear this hospital gown at night to sleep. They took your clothes and put them in with everybody else's clothes in this thing called a hot box, and when you got 'em back in the morning, they smelled like everybody else's clothes. That was disgusting.

So I moved onto the streets, and I've pretty much been living outside ever since. Including the wintertime. If you have the right gear, you'd be amazed at what you can survive.

I usually don't have a problem with the cops. You know where Irving Park is? You know the clock tower there? I used to sleep under there in the wintertime. This one cop got to know me pretty good, and he'd usually pull in about one o'clock in the morning, bring me some sandwiches and some hot soup. He'd sit there and talk with me. He was really a nice guy.

There's a preserve right there, and there's a lot of raccoons that live in there. Some of them are really big—25-,

30-pounders. I used to feed them every night. One night—it was really a cold night—I fed them, and I went over and set up my stuff, and I laid down.

About two hours later, it felt like a body laid down beside me. I popped up out of my bag and pulled my blanket back. Two raccoons laid longways right beside me. They stayed there till like four o'clock in the morning. They were keeping me warm. Swear to God it's a true story.

I don't need money. I've had it before, and it didn't do me any good. I don't need to worry about food or clothing, 'cause there's always somehow, some way that it comes through. I can go three, four days without eating, and I'm still okay.

One Sunday I'm sitting in Welles Park waiting for the library to open. This guy walked up. He said to me, "Are you homeless?" I said, "Yeah." He said, "How can you handle it?" I said, "Well, homelessness is not for everybody. Why, are you thinking about it?" He says, "I'm so confused." He goes "Here," and he hands me $20. Then he says, "No, here," and he hands me 40 more bucks. Then he goes, "No, here," and he hands me three $100 bills, and I had to push him away, cause he was going to open up his wallet and hand me more money. I walked away, and I said "God, what was this about?"

At night when I lay down, I'm a lonely guy. At times. But then at other times, I go to lay down at night and I don't feel so lonely. I'm just the only one there.

"EMMA"

I started coming to church about 1999. That's when the pantry was very small. It wasn't something that interested me. Then two years, three years later, one day there was a woman who was leaving All Saints to go to New York for some job. She talked about what goes on here, and she talked with tears. I said, "Gosh, I want to check out what moved her like that."

I came the very next Tuesday. There used to be couches here in the parish hall, and I sat on the couch, scared to death. This guy started talking to me. He was loud and abrasive, and we got along. Then the next week I looked for him, and he was here.

Then I fell madly in love with Reverend Bridget, because she was the start of it all. To me, she was like a female Jesus. I just loved how I felt when I was around her. She had this brand-new baby, a brand-new baby boy, and she'd let anybody in here hold him and talk to him and stick their dirty hands on his cheeks.

I remember when our numbers were almost going to hit 100, and Bridget would sit out here crying, going, "I don't know what we're going to do." I'd tell her, "Don't worry about it! We'll figure it out!"

I never in a million years thought I would have friends that were homeless or that were not all right in the head. Now I could pop probably to every single table and have a conversation with somebody. "How was your week?" That's how I start every conversation. "How was your week?

What did you do? How was your Thanksgiving?"

Our lives aren't that different, is what I've learned the most. The difference is in the way they communicate. They don't really have phones. Some of them don't read, so they don't have newspapers. Everything has to be verbal communication. It's like that old game we used to play as kids, Telephone.

I try to seek out certain individuals every single week, because I want to make sure that I touch them. It's very important, touch. They don't get touched a lot. They get scorned a lot. So I hug and I touch and I kiss. I never talk to anybody without touching them unless I know they've got phobias.

I really like [this one woman]. I don't know why we connected. Like, our souls just liked each other. I'm not trying to make myself sound special. I think some people just connect and some people don't.

She's not on the street anymore, but she used to be. Around Memorial Day I wanted to know what it was like to be homeless. So I asked her, "Can I hang with you all weekend and see what your life is like?" Well, she couldn't be happier. That was the most fascinating day of my life. It still chokes me up sometimes when I talk about it. We went down to the lake and she showed me all her haunts. We stood in line like she would do for lunch and for dinner.

Everybody wants to volunteer around Christmas because it's the thing to do. It's my personal feeling that that sucks. That's really sad, that you want to do it once a year because it's the thing to do. To do it because you think they need help grates on me. I do it for friendship.

Everybody always points new volunteers to me and says, "Tell 'em what you do up here in the parish hall." I always say, "Talk to 'em. Just talk to 'em." There's nothing you can do for 'em. Just talk to 'em, reach out to them, be a friend. Be a friend. That's all I do. It makes me happy to be here, and I think everybody here is happy to be here. If it was a sad place, there's no way I could walk through these doors all the time.

I'm the most shy person you'll ever meet. Nobody knows that but my partner. I'm extremely shy. It looks like I'm very social, right? No, I'm scared to death. I was very frightened when I got here. I'm never frightened at all anymore. I am so charged when I leave. I have a hard time sleeping at night on Tuesdays because I'm charged up.

I don't seek God. God is just with me. I don't have to worry about it or think about it. It's not that deep for me. I'm very shallow.

Glen

GLEN

I've always been the soft, effeminate guy. I relate so much better and easier to the girls. It's just the state of mind I was born into.

This summer I'm planning on going to community college. I want to study business administration. An immediate goal for me is just to get my bank account straight and get me a place to sleep at night. I'm safe for tonight. I'm staying in a shelter. I hope it's the last time I'll be in a shelter.

Some people call me crazy. With the medication, I get the sleep I need, and when I get the sleep I need, I know where I'm at. But insomnia brings on this altered state of mind.

With these psychotic experiences, if you come in contact with me when I'm in one of 'em, realize that I'm sick, I'm on the way to the hospital, and in my reality, I'm with Jesus. Somewhere along the line, Jesus came to me and said, "Let's go, Glen." Well, who knows? He might need me to do something.

I'm fine with God. It's me and myself that I have problems with. I can't get my medicine, because I don't have an ID card. Well, I can't get my ID card because my bank account is toast. So I have to wait till I get my Social Security check, which has been three weeks tomorrow. And I got everything paper-wise except the $20 bill.

I want God, money, and beautiful women. Not necessarily in that order.

Ahn

Ed

Beau

BEAU

I am originally from Jackson, Tennessee, which is in the western part of Tennessee, near Memphis. I am an only child.

I grew up Southern Baptist, but my parents were not picky about making me going to church. I didn't like church because everyone was affluent, and we were not. I always felt not good enough. So I just didn't like church until I was about 12 or 13. After that, I got to be a little more accepted, because I came into my own as a musician.

I remember, when I was in kindergarten, thinking this other guy who was on the slide was cute. I didn't think anything else about it.

I came out when I was 17. It really was not traumatic. I sat down with my mom first. She said, "Oh, I've known since you were two." Then I had the conversation with my dad. I think he cried.

When I first got the Internet, it gave me a chance to talk to people who were gay. I had no other way to do that. At all. I happened to start chatting with Steve one night on instant messenger. We just talked and talked. He was a person who, I don't think, ever really thought he'd find somebody to be in a long-term relationship with. I was, too.

The first time we met in person, afterwards, he asked me to marry him. I said, "I really have no idea what I'm doing, but yes." It was the right thing to do. As the years go by, we find more and more ways where we gel.

CASEY

I was having a really shitty day. I had just had my wallet stolen. So I decided rather than sitting at home or going to a bar, I'd take a walk. My walk led me over here to church, and I knew it was pantry night, but I didn't really know anything about it. I walked up and I said, "Do you need help?" and this volunteer looked at me and said, "Yes! Come here! Pass out milk!"

Being the milk lady is a fun job. They give me their tickets. Then I give them milk and, when we have it, juice. Unfortunately we have lots of grapefruit juice, and lots of people don't like grapefruit juice, specially if you're on medication. But you know, I can give them a smile and wish them a nice night.

When I worked in the Lincoln Park neighborhood, I was treated like a shop girl on a daily basis, like I probably had the IQ of a newt. I'd still smile at them, and yet I'd get the stony face back. That happens less frequently here, that I'm greeted with no smile or a don't-look-me-in-the-eye type thing.

It's funny—I had made such a pilgrimage away from my faith. It's amazing to feel like I am part of something again. I was a theology major at a Catholic university, and due to disgruntled feelings with the Catholic church, stepped away from it for a long time. The Catholic church ticks me off with their whole stance on gays. Anyone who knows me knows that 90 percent of my friends are gay, lesbian, bi, something.

I look forward to this all week. My kids look forward to it, and they fight over who can go. My youngest is really angry that she hasn't been able to come yet, but I think she's too little. The other one likes to be all over the place. She thinks she owns it. She's six and a half. Sometimes she helps me with milk, though she likes to be in the kitchen. She likes to scrape the dessert plates a lot.

Sometimes you'll hear her say, "Do you think that guy doesn't have a house?," and it's like, "Let's be a little bit more sensitive." But that's why we live in the city. We didn't move to lily-white land, because I don't want my kids to not know that there are people who are hungry in our neighborhood.

There was a man who lived in our bus stop for a while, and the girls were upset, because it was starting to get really cold. So we brought him a blanket. Because we walk by him every day. You can't walk by him and not say hello. You can't walk by and not look this gentleman in the eye.

"LARRY"

When I first came around, I started just going to services. Then I started volunteering on Tuesday. Helping other people because I wanted to for no reason at all. That's it. Does there have to be a reason for everything? I just like coming here. If I come here just so I can die and go to heaven, that's not a good reason for coming, is it?

I was Swedish Covenant. My dad was a missionary. I spent five and a half years in Taiwan and went to missionary boarding school. If they were Christians, I hoped once in a while that I wasn't. One was a Free Methodist. You never want to tangle with a Free Methodist.

I never enjoyed going to church when my father was preaching. "Boy, you're going to get a spanking as soon as we get home." And out would come the razor strop. That kind of religion.

If you're bipolar, you're bipolar all your life. You know where the bridge is, the overpass that went underneath the old post office? I got up there somehow, and I wanted to get down by the water. I guess I was going to jump, and I could literally hear a voice: "Oh! My, my, my. You don't want to jump. You might hurt yourself."

Then another voice said, "Well, you want to get down there. It looks like the only way you're going to get down there is to jump. Why don't you try it and see what happens?"

After about half an hour of that, I told them both to shut

up. I was real calm, everything was really nice, and I said, "I want to get down there," and I jumped. I shattered my ankles.

I was never mad about it or angry at myself about it. I never said it was stupid, like some people would. It was just something I did. It was logical, with my state of mind.

If somebody called me crazy, I'd say, "Yeah, and I got the paperwork to prove it." I'm crazy, but at least I know it, and I'm doing something about it. My thinking has finally slowed down. For the most part, I enjoy myself. I read a lot. Walk around a lot. Get on the computer. See friends. Sit around coffee shops. I just wish they hadn't raised the prices for the museum tickets that high.

I just take it as it comes, because I don't have to make plans any more. Isn't that the trouble with the world? So many people want to accomplish something, and some of them manage it.

Fran

FRAN

It was fun to come out when I did. Nowadays, you go to the gay pride parade, and it feels like one big bar party. But back then, it was a really radical thing to be going out on the street and marching. There was something very fun about that, something very dangerous and exciting and fun. I still have a major rebel streak.

I grew up in the Austin neighborhood, right outside Oak Park. Back then, it was very white, a middle-class working neighborhood. I went to this Catholic girl's school, and they offered women's studies, which was pretty radical in 1976. I discovered feminist literature and feminist theology and all these wonderful books by lesbian authors.

It was then that my eyes opened up and I came out to myself. I was kind of scared. Back then, you could not tell people on your job that you were gay. You could not *get* a job if people knew you were gay. In high school I continued to date this guy who I hung out with, just 'cause it was like, "Okay, this is the kind of thing I gotta be doing."

Right after high school, I was doing volunteer work with the National Organization for Women. That's where I met my partner, Eileen. We moved in together in 1980. I had just turned 20 years old. And we've been living together ever since.

It's in some ways strange to me, because I've always struggled with my self-esteem, ever since I was a child and even through my whole adulthood. But I've never struggled with being gay. That is the one thing that I have always really loved about myself. And I wouldn't change it.

I have always felt, since high school, that I was called to be a priest. I really believe it was a call from God, because it never went away, no matter what else I did. I finally decided: I have got to follow this. I have got to find the right denomination and the right church and follow this.

I told my parents I was a lesbian probably after Eileen and I had lived together a couple years. They were not very happy about it. My mother didn't really like to talk about it, but one year for Christmas she gave us a brand-new quilt for our bed, and that was her way of giving us something as a couple. And actually, when my mother was dying, Eileen took care of her. She would let Eileen do things for her that me and my sister couldn't do for her. Eileen was going to nursing school, so I think she felt comfortable with her: "Yeah, let her give me the injection of heparin."

It's surprising to people how many of our neighbors [at the food pantry] are gay. I've had a couple of them talk to me about it. Then they feel, "Oh, okay, so I can come to this church. I can be a part of this place."

We try to provide nutritious meals for people. I think everybody deserves that. They come in here and get a moment of rest and relaxation. My favorite part of Tuesday night is talking to the neighbors when they're first coming in. Especially if we have a really good dinner planned that I know they're going to enjoy. Like if we're having roast beef, mashed potatoes, vegetables, and dessert—they're all over that.

I'm always aware of different neighbors and things they're trying to do, whether it's get into a job program or finish school or get housing. I want to help them in any way that I can, but I also know for some of them, it just might not work out. And I don't want them to feel that if it hasn't worked out that I think ill of them, or that they can't come back here. 'Cause we all have things in life that don't work out.

There's a part of me that always thinks: "Let's not put overimportance on what we do in the scheme of their life." It's important to me to treat people with dignity and respect and welcome them and give them a good meal, and make sure that while they're here, we do what we can do for them. But I also don't want to have an unrealistic view of our place in their world. Many of these people have survived incredible things, and it wasn't 'cause of us, you know? It's just a place. One night a week, it's just someplace where somebody knows them. And I think you just have to be okay with that.

I have things that I do away from the church. I take vacation. I take time with family. I just went to the spa Friday; that's why I have this crazy green nail polish on. It's on my toes also. Someone gave me a gift certificate to the spa, so I had the whole package. And then they're like, "What color nail polish do you want?" I'm like, "No one's ever asked me that question."

"DONNA"

I was in LA, and I was out there with a friend of mine who had a music studio, and I was thinking maybe I would move out there. I was in a lot of turmoil in my life. I didn't know what to do. I really didn't feel loved, and I didn't feel connected, and I was a lost soul.

I was biding my time, waiting for my redeye home. I was at Tower Records on Sunset, wasting time. There was something playing on the sound system. I was into recording at the time, sound engineering. I was hearing this reverb. I'm like, "Wow, that's the Lexicon 200 they're using on that voice." It was this new reverb that had just come out.

I go up to the guy at the counter. I go, "What is that?" He goes, "It's this," and he throws down the cassette. I bought it so I could listen on the plane. I had one of the first Walkmans ever that were out. I'm on the plane, and I'm playing this cassette. All of a sudden, I'm hearing: "Falling down all around us, love has lit a fire."

I'm like, "What?" Then I pull out the insert, and I'm reading the lyrics, going, "What the hell is this? What is this?" And then I hear something about Jesus, and I'm rewinding it. "What is that? What is that?" I looped the thing over and over and over the whole flight. Four and a half hours, it just keeps playing, this crazy cassette. It's Amy Grant. I just start crying after about the fifth time through. This one song just kept playing, and it just went to my soul. This hunger and this fire, everything.

I got back to life in Chicago. And I hid that cassette. I just put that cassette, like, *away*: "I don't know what that thing is." I'm like, "I'm busy, I'm busy, I'm busy." And always I could feel. I could feel Jesus and the love of Jesus Christ calling me. Calling out from around me. Love has lit a fire.

I'm very comfortable around alcoholics and people that might be messy, including myself. I talk to everyone. I talk to the clerk at the store. [On Tuesday nights] I just walk around and talk and listen and catch up with people. I try to be a constant presence. There's always just seems like there's somebody who needs some encouragement. Or I'll get encouraged by somebody. It works both ways. I don't see it as being some supernatural feat. I just think we should open the door and people should come in and we should give 'em what we have here.

If you have an agenda here, you'll go crazy. If you have an agenda that you're going to transform lives or whatever the hell it is you're going to do—No. I get to say hi to some people. I get to hug 10 people. They're going to tell me some stories; they're going to catch me up, they're going to tell me crazy stuff, I'm going to tell them crazy stuff. And then we'll clean it all up, put the chairs away, put the tables up.

That is the powerful thing we can do, is just love people. I'm not here to teach people. I'm here to love them. And I think that loving people is what teaches them. Maybe that's fudging it. But that's my story. And I'm sticking to it.

JOE

I always had this thing where I wanted to be a doctor. Me being a doctor is about as realistic as me flying, academically. But I always wanted to help people.

I was doing some work on my friend's house. On Tuesdays, she'd say, "I have to get down to the church." Finally I said, "What are you doing?" She described what was going on. So I said, "I'll try two Tuesdays and that's it. It wouldn't be practical for me to come out here every week." It's about 65 miles one way. Three years later, here I am.

Every week I get here about 4:15, 4:30. I usually bring the milk up. I make sure somebody's doing the bags. I go upstairs and make sure that somebody's doing the coffee and the lemonade. And I open up the door and let the people in.

I grew up Back of the Yards, on the South Side. Fifty-first and Bishop. A tough neighborhood. Very poor. My dad was an alcoholic. My grandmother owned the house we lived in, and thank God, because I think she forgave rent payments. We didn't have a car. You didn't go anywhere, you didn't do anything.

Our house was just turmoil. I left when I was 22, and the reason I waited so long was, my dad was dying of cancer. I was the only person in the house besides him who drove, so I had to keep driving him to the veterans' hospital and chemo. Finally I did move out, and a year later he died.

I got accepted to Loyola, which I never thought I would. I

was there for two years, and after that, Loyola asked me to leave, because I couldn't keep up—I was working practically full-time. I went to University of Illinois in Chicago. I did that for a year. Finally I just dropped out. I was kind of lost. One of my friends from the old neighborhood started telling me about Larkin Home. It's a facility that works with emotionally disturbed kids. The more he talked, the more I wanted to be there.

So I worked in the intensive care unit, where the kids were really severely emotionally damaged. Then they needed somebody to go out to this group home. So I transferred over there. Then I started training people to work with emotionally disturbed kids. And then I could be a supervisor if I got my bachelor's, so I had to go back to school. I was 33, and I finally got my degree. It took me 17 years.

When the kids were sweet, it was really neat. You knew they were going to turn on you. One minute they're saying how much they love you, and they hope you're always going to be here, and the next minute it was, "I hope you die, and your parents die, and your friends die, and your girlfriend dies." The next day they'd go, "Sorry." You see through that, and you see it's the person there that needs help, that's hurting.

It reminds me a little bit of one of the patrons here—she cursed me out cause I didn't get something for her. The next week she came back and said, "Sorry. Sorry about I said." If you keep your heart open, you know, you get that.

Bonnie

Gale

Mary

MARY

I've always been trying to figure out my place in life. And I can't figure it out. But I've always liked people. I've always wanted to help. Going through school and going through church—it's deepened that. The more I go, the deeper it gets.

I was a CNA [certified nursing assistant]. We weren't able to do much—just be with people and talk to them and read to them. A woman's father was in there for a heart attack. Months later, she recognized me. I didn't know who she was, but she gave me the biggest hug and told me that even though I didn't do much, that that really meant something to him and to her family. And it just, like, brought me to tears.

I decided I wanted to go full time to nursing school. I'm going into my third semester. I would like to be a certified registered nurse anesthetist, but that's way up there. I'd be happy with just being an associate-degree registered nurse. Blood, needles, none of that bothers me.

I'm not in nursing school technically. I'm taking my general eds. I just got through taking a basic writing course, and I took a music theory course, which was just too hard, and I ended up failing the class, so I'm on probation. But that's okay. I'll make up for it.

I'm a Christian, and I really, really want to do something for my Lord. If He gave me this desire, well, I think that's what I'm supposed to do. I can't think of anything else. I've tried waitressing. I've tried cashiering. I worked at the airport. To me, it's like, anybody can do that. I want something with some meat to it.

I've been divorced since '86. We had two kids. I miscarried one—it would have been three. James is my oldest, and then I have a daughter. My son is kind of learning-disabled, so for him to live on his own would be really hard. But the Lord assured me he's going to be okay, no matter what happens. And that's hard to put your trust in. But I just do.

James, he's been working at Dominick's for 11 years. He pushes carts, he bags groceries. He has such a good time there, and they know him really well. He likes to run. He likes to swing on swings. He likes to give hugs and compliments. He has the gift of help and hospitality.

Growing up, it was like I had a sign: "Bother me." I have been shot at, I've had a gun pulled on me. I was raped at knifepoint the day after my 30th birthday. Without God, I would have been dead a long time ago. But he keeps me going.

All my life, I was trying to do good things just to get on His good side. I was trying to, like, prove myself. You don't have to prove yourself. I didn't know that. What Jesus did on the cross, he paid for everything. I was like, wow. It was an eye-opener.

MIKE

I wanted my degree in oceanography, because I wanted to go swim with fish. It just didn't happen. Not for me it didn't.

I do odd-and-end jobs just to keep money in my pocket. But I always stay working, no matter what. Sometimes I go two, three days without sleep because I'm always bouncing from one job to the next. I have the cleaning job going, the shoveling job going, the plowing job going, plus I'm a part-time laborer for the Allstate Arena.

I'm falling short of money. I need things to pick up real quick real fast. This guy I'm working for tomorrow, he changed the time on me again. They change just when I have everything set. As long as I'm done by 10 o'clock so I can hit my 11:30, I'm okay, but now my 11:30 might turn to 12.

I went to college. The first year just didn't cut it for me. My first class was at 6:15. I got out of that class at 10 after 7. I had to be at the other side of the campus by 7:35. You can't do it in 25 minutes. There's just no possible way unless you have a bike, and I didn't have anything.

I raised a 17-year-old boy by myself. Me and my son, we are in St. Louis, Missouri. I bought a trailer for $9,500. We've been out there for three years now. I bounce back and forth [between there and Chicago], but I have good friends here that I stay with every single night. I do not sleep on the streets. I was out there for almost two years. It's not for me.

I have less than six months before my kid goes off to college. My great-great-grandmother left me money to give to my kid, if I ever had one. So he's got money for college; I'm not worried about that. I just gotta keep him in there. I'm going to have to do my damndest to make sure he does not get discouraged.

What's to think about Barack Obama? He made it. Wow. Whoopy-doo. I don't care who's president, and I don't care who's mayor. They are not putting money in my pocket. I'm out there working just like any other working-class person out there, and I'm making my money. These guys ain't doing nothing for me. I'm doing for myself. Ain't nothing to worry about. I'm on my job.

ROB

I grew up in Robert Taylor Homes. That's on State Street between 39th and 55th streets. It's no longer there. My dad was a working-class guy, and so was my mom. They ain't got time to sit down and have that cool talk that settles all things. They come from the old school, like, "Dude, I got to go to work tomorrow, and I work hard. I'm tired." But I didn't think about the big picture. I'm thinking about how come I don't have Converses. You know what I'm saying. Stupid stuff. Kid-thinking stuff.

But we soldiered through. They showed a little fortitude and tried to make a way for us. We did that moving-on-up, Jeffersons, *Good Times* thing, out of the projects and into our home. And we all did our part.

You never know what light you may shine on somebody. Mine happened in eighth grade. I was sitting in class, and somebody left a note on my desk that said my mother was a green hornet. Now I had low self-esteem, because I had failed sixth grade. I was already conditioned to be in last place, not to be included in anything, not to be a part of the basketball game, the softball game, go to the party. This was just the straw that broke the camel's back. So I ran to the bathroom and started crying.

During those days, teachers could smoke in the boys' bathroom. So my teacher, Mr. Robinson, is in there smoking a cigarette asking me what's wrong, and I told him what happened. And he said, "Why you worrying about them, what they said about your mother? You the smartest kid in the class."

Now I don't know if he told that to every kid in the class. But I choose not to care. And I chose not to care because that's the best thing I heard that day. It was a keeper. I kept that with me.

I hadn't been the smartest kid in anything, and I had a record to prove it. But since he told me that, I had to believe it. When he told me that, I worked at being the smartest kid in the class, because he gave me an identity other than the kid that got beat up on the schoolyard and made C grades. And then after that I was, like, first in everything, or in the top 10 percent. He assigned me a new life. All my teachers were surprised to see that I came out first. I was surprised too.

My grandfather, his name was Buddy Wilson. He was from the old school, the '20s. Him and my grandmom, they kept it really conservative. They were conservative black folks. He had got word that I was doing really well in school. I had hand-me-downs and stuff from the resale shop my whole time in grammar school with a few new things sprinkled here and there, 'cause my parents were saving for a house; they couldn't just buy new stuff all the time.

So he told me, "If you do well coming out of school, I'm going to buy you a suit." I'm figuring I'm gonna go to Sears. That's like the Marshall Fields of poor people.

He takes me to Moore Cooper. That was on State Street. It's not there anymore. They measured me, and they cut me a suit. I walked out of there with something that the kids on the Gold Coast would wear. Tie, shirt, everything.

Nothing fabulous. All business. And I've been all business ever since.

I got time for Christ now. A few years ago, I would have said, "Get out of my face, dude. I make enough money, I got enough friends, who are you to tell me anything?" But now I'm encouraged spiritually. My dreams validate that I'm on the right path. And I am. A few of my dreams and visions came true.

So I've been canvassing people whenever I get an opportunity: "Tell me a dream." I usually trade dreams. I give 'em a couple of dreams that I had, and then usually that opens up the dike. You'd be amazed how many similar dreams that people have. It's an indication that He poured his spirit on all His children.

I'm still a prodigal son, don't get me wrong. I'm still a Luke 15 guy. I was more scoundrel than honorable man. I loved my carnal life. I ain't gonna lie. I loved my nice car, nice parties, bar stools, and oh, and the Jezebels that sat around me. I was a hard sell for Christ.

But the Lord said we're the light of the earth and the salt of the world, and I have to believe it. If I believe Mr. Robinson, then I have to believe Christ. So I study my book. I have to work at understanding what the smartest kid in the class is in God's class. I'm not the smartest kid on earth, and nobody's ever told me I was the smartest person that they ever met. Well, a few girlfriends did. But they was just trying to get a little closer.

Julie

JULIE

I was a psychiatric nurse for a long time. We set up a clinic here, and it's fabulous. We started out doing blood pressures and weights and a lot of health teaching. Then we began looking for places we could send people, because we don't prescribe medications.

These people are just a sea of unmet health care needs. There are agencies that in theory provide care to them, but getting them connected is incredibly difficult. There's one agency that says you have to have an official note that you're homeless. Isn't that fabulous?

I had a lady who had terrifyingly high blood pressure, and she finally is going to see somebody and taking medication. There was a lady with really bad pain in her knees, and I was able to say, "You need to keep moving. You have arthritis in your knees. If you sit, it will get worse. You do need to walk some, maybe put warm packs on your knees." I get some satisfaction that they know somebody cares about them and checks on them.

I have the luxury of treating people as whole human beings, which is very nice. One guy I know is real worried about his brother, who's been very sick, so I ask him about that. A nurse practitioner in a white lab coat and a stethoscope would just be treating illness.

I have a terrible time remembering people's names, but I don't have a hard time remembering the names of the people here. I don't know what that says about me.

I'm not really certain that there's a God at all. I kind of lean against it, but it's just very comfortable for me. Is there a God? Was Christ somehow a member of the Trinity? I don't care anymore. All this seems to work philosophically and aesthetically and culturally and morally and politically and every other way. I'm happy here, so if I drop over dead and nothing happens, big deal. I'll be dead.

It's really rude to mentally ill people to say, "Oh, they don't take their meds." No, they don't, but neither does anybody else. When you look at the national data on long-term adherence to any medication, it is not terribly good. I'm impressed with some of the people I see who are very good about taking their medications. The medications for schizophrenia have gotten much better. A lot of people say, "I feel so much better. The voices are so much less."

I think a lot about this: Am I satisfied with too little? The small bits of success that I have, I think, can be falsely self-congratulatory: "Oh, isn't that nice that so and-so happened." When in reality, this person's diabetes isn't under control, or their high blood pressure isn't under control.

A guy comes in and he says, "My legs are all swollen, and they're very painful." I said, "Can you prove you're homeless?" He said, "No, I can't. I'm in from Vegas." I said, "I can give you the name of a clinic." And then he said, "Oh, I'm coughing up blood." I said, "What you need to do is go to Weiss, to their emergency room. Bring something to read; it'll take you hours to be seen. Tell them you're coughing up blood." I felt like, "Oh, I'm a good person, providing this helpful information."

And as I'm driving home, I'm seeing him and his friend walking east on Wilson. It fully dawns on me how far it is from here to Weiss. What an incredibly long walk for someone whose legs are his chief complaint. His painful, swollen legs. And that's what I've done for him.

Whoopy-doo. You know? Whoopy-do. The best I could do for him is send him on a mile-and-a-half walk of pain to an emergency room where they won't want to see him. And this is the best we're doing? That stinks. Oh, it really bothered me. I still think about seeing that man walking down the street.

Sylvester

SYLVESTER

I met a guy in high school that turned me onto rock music. At first I didn't really too much care for Jimi Hendrix. His sound didn't do nothin' for me. I thought he was just wild. But when I saw the Woodstock movie, that kind of changed my whole outlook. The band I really liked was Led Zepplin, 'cause I got a chance to see them at the Chicago Stadium when I was real young. Best thing that happened to me.

I wanted to learn how to play guitar, but a strange thing happened when I got out of high school. I was with a friend. He was drag racing, and his brakes gave out on him, and it almost tore my hand off. That's the reason I don't drive. It took a while for me to even try to use this hand. That was my dream out the window.

My son, right now I'm trying to get him into learning how to play. He's 11. He saw this Guitar Hero thing, so he wants to. I said, "Well, you'll have that for Christmas, but you've gotta learn how to be dedicated if you want to learn how to play." If he wants to learn anything, I got a lot of cassette tapes, but I got a lot of albums, too. I still have the stuff that I have from the '70s all the way up to now. I just don't buy albums no more, 'cause CDs is the wave now.

I always had this theory—I'm a conspiracy theorist—that during the Roswell thing in New Mexico, space monsters came down here, and that's why we got all that TV technology. I'm not sure of the radio, but the TV technology and the cell phones and stuff, that came from the space monsters. That's my theory. Everybody's entitled to an opinion. I see people just staring at their cell phone. It's like, there's nobody calling, they staring at it. I don't get it.

Where I work at is, we do albums for photographers. Last year was the first year that I ever got a chance to work a computer. One guy left and they didn't want to bring no guy from the agency in, so they threw me in. Took me about three weeks to learn it. The baddest thing about my job is, they let the union go. I'm doing maybe three or four jobs. You can't complain, 'cause you have people getting laid off. And now they're talking about we not going to get no raise the first of the year 'cause they not making no money, which I think is a bunch of crap.

But I do okay. Compared to some of the people that's here, I do okay. Sometimes, like last week, I didn't even eat at all [at the food pantry]. 'Cause I don't eat pasta. Anytime they have pasta, I don't eat. I had money on me, so I felt, well, let somebody else get that plate.

I hate holidays, 'cause of people's expectations of how things should be on them holidays. If you look at how many holidays we celebrate, I think maybe they should cut some things out. I mean, July 4th is cool, Thanksgiving is cool, Christmas is cool. New Year's is what I like. You coming into the year. You don't really need no resolution for what you gotta do. Just come into the year and say, "Hey, if I don't get a chance to do it, I'll get around to doing it."

You ever get that feeling, there's something else you want to do, but you can't pinpoint it? I had this little idea. When I was a little boy, my dad used to take me to a place called the Regal Theater out on 37th. They used to have a lot of the acts—the Temptations, Otis Redding, Ike and Tina Turner, Bobby Bland.

I said, "Well, they gonna come out with the Chess Brothers and make a movie on them, I think they maybe should make a movie on how it feels to be at the Regal Theatre seeing all these acts in the 60s." It's something that's been crossing my mind, but I would have to go all the way back in my brain to figure out how would you write it.

Sam

SAM

I went to high school and grammar school on the northwest side of Chicago, and after that, I tried about a year of college at DePaul for business administration. Unfortunately I didn't have the brains for it, or the money.

I always had the idea in my mind that I would be the white Mike Tyson. At this point, my career as a boxer has pretty much come to an end. They said if I take any more concussions to the skull, I could bleed out from inside my brain, and that's certainly no good. I used to be a heavyweight. I've dropped close to 100 pounds in the last five years.

I boxed all over the United States for a while. I boxed in Branson, Missouri—that's like the Vegas of the South. I boxed here in Chicago, in nightclubs, small clubs. About the most notable place I ever boxed was the O'Hare Hilton. I never won a title. My days of being kicked in the head for a living are pretty much over.

I'm not a friendly person. I occasionally enjoy talking to people. Sometimes people take what I say the wrong way, but I don't mean any harm. I don't bite. At this point I've kind of given up on friends as a general practice.

I love animals. Right now, I have a cat. I got Loolak from a Serbian gentleman with a crack problem. He sold me this cat for $20, and this cat was dehydrated when I got it—its ribs were poking out. I really got this animal back from the brink of death. He's a sweet cat. I like my little kitty.

I'm one of these people who sits around and watches TV

a lot. Mainly what I watch is sporting events and news programs, like *48 Hours, Dateline*. Investigative reporting shows. You can learn something from those.

As for God and religion now, I don't attend church services on a regular basis. The church I'm involved in most would be something called the Shepherd's Chapel out of Arkansas. They're a television ministry. I buy their teachings and tapes sometimes over the TV. In my opinion, they're the only church that really teaches the truth. The man who runs it, Pastor Murray, is very highly educated. I really like him, because he can document every single thing that he says from the Bible. They don't talk in tongues, they just go straight on with teaching the Bible line by line, verse by verse.

I think everyone should make the world a better place. There are so many other people making the world a nasty place.

LORI

My father worked for Commonwealth Edison. When we were kids, we used to say, "What do you do, Dad?" He'd say, "I watch the coal pile." We never knew until he was retiring that he was boss of the Fifth Street station. I had two brothers, and of course they're both gone now. I'll be 86 in September.

I married one of the guys I went to high school with. First we lived in the Elinor Hotel at Cicero and Belmont. Then my husband got drafted.

Anybody that was in the Army, Navy, Marines, Coast Guard, the government would put you in an apartment in Cabrini Green. I think we paid $40 a month. At that time it was a bunch of Army servicemen's wives. There was blacks, there was Filipinos, there was everything. And the kids got along fine. The only time there'd be a fight is if they were playing baseball or something: "That was a home run!" "No, it wasn't! You were out!" The kids'd take their bat and ball, and everybody'd go home.

When my younger son was little, I got a job at Brach's, and he stayed with his babysitter, who was black. Pearl and Arthur Smith. They lived in the apartment upstairs. And he used to love his Pearl. He thought every day he had to go and eat with them, even Sundays, Saturdays.

We used to go shopping at—I think it was the A&P then, on LaSalle Street. We'd walk over there, and Arthur would put Michael on his shoulder. There used to be a man that we'd see there every time we would go, and he was bald, but he had hair in the back. So he used to take that hair and comb it forward and put a rubber band around his hair. We used to die laughing. We didn't let him see, but it was hilarious.

When we first moved in there, I think I wore a size 10 in a girl's dress. I was down shootin' marbles with the kids and turning the jump rope and doing everything. I used to be 5 foot 1, and now I'm 4 foot 8.

My husband's mother worked for Salerno, the cookie place. She used to give us cookies by the ton. I told my children, "You never go out and eat a cookie in front of a bunch of kids that are looking at you. You either eat it in the house, or you bring enough out for all the kids." So we got rid of a bunch of Salerno butter cookies, let me tell you, because every kid had to get one.

We got along until my husband got out of the Navy. He didn't like the life he was living, and we finally got divorced. It was a good thing that we got a divorce, because my 15-year-old son told my husband, "If you hit my mother one more time, there's going to be big trouble." I told my husband, "That's it," because why should my son beat his father up or kill him for a mistake that I made? My kids told me later, "You never should have stayed with him." I learned that.

I worked at Brach's for a long time, and I was a good worker. I was a fast worker, thank God. Years ago, before we got big machines, we used to do everything by hand. You'd take a fancy box, turn it upside down, fold the cellophane over it, and you had a glue brush, and you would hand-seal it.

We used to make these dessert mints. I said, "Why don't we call 'em confetti mints?" That made them say, "Hey, we need you in the R&D lab, research and development." So that's where I went, and I was there until I quit. I was one of the last ones to go out the door because I had senior-ity. Fifty-six years. I can't look at a mint anymore. Yuck! I wouldn't give you a nickel for a ton.

If I don't feel good, I go stay with my son for a couple of days, 'cause he worries that I'm gonna fall down. He lives in Edison Park. He was out of work for a long time, honey. For a long time. I got a big bonus when I quit work because I had 50 years in. Went through that like nothin' cause I was paying his mortgage for about seven years. What am I gonna do, pile it up in the bank and say, "Look at all the money I got?" Uh-uh. You give it to 'em when they need it.

Michael

MICHAEL

It seemed to happen pretty quickly. My wife went in for a colonoscopy, and they said they found something that they didn't like. They were concerned that if it were left unchecked, it would grow into cancer. They took the lower part of her colon out to remove the spot and make sure they'd gotten everything. The prognosis was all very good. Of course you sit down and talk to the gastroenterologist who's doing the surgery. Well, in some small percentage of cases, less than two percent, you can have a leak develop. Okay, so two percent. That's not going to happen, right?

After the surgery is over, she seemed fine. She was about ready to be released, and she just kept on feeling weird. Her white count looks fine; everything looks fine. They kept on taking all these blood tests. Nope, no problem, no problem. Well, as it turns out, she and her sister share this attribute that everything looks fine until disaster is about to set in. Well, that's what happened with her. They noticed that there was a leak. She was becoming septic. There was no time to react. You're kind of left with: Huh?

They took her into surgery right away and tried to clean up as much as they could and sew her back up. The doctor explained what happened and said she's going to be in a coma for a while. He said that she had acute respiratory distress syndrome, ARDS, and he said, "Look it up on the internet." I looked it up. Well, it wasn't good. They talk about percentage of people that live through it. Sixty percent survive. That's not a good number. I want it to be 99.99 percent. I started crying, which I rarely do.

I mean, it was bad. She was on life support. They had 11 tubes running in and out of her. They found the best way to reduce the problems with ARDS is to keep the patient moving. So they have you in this bed that rotates. The nurse comes in every 45 minutes and flips her over. So part of the time, she was looking down—well, she wasn't looking down, 'cause she was asleep—and part of the time, she was face up. And they have to move those tubes every time that happens.

She's absolutely, completely back now. No difference.

Even though it seems like I should be this way, I always have difficulty talking about God and faith and that sort of stuff. Maybe I'm a good Episcopalian that way. Even though clearly I do believe all that sort of stuff.

"ANDY"

I'm from a little ol' town called Gideon, Missouri, but I lived in Texas almost all my life. Came to Chicago getting away from my ex-wife. I said, "The furthest place I can get from her, the better I like it."

I packed up my little California suitcase—which in street talk is a little box wrapped around with a belt—and I put it in an old truck I used to have, and I drove all the way from Dallas, Texas, all the way up to Chicago. I left her with a two-bedroom house, a brand-new truck, and two and a half acres of land.

I didn't know nobody. I didn't have nothing. When I first got here, I slept on the streets a couple of times. I said, "Well, this ain't the thing for me." Now I stay at the Wilson Hotel. It ain't the best in the West, but it's a roof over my head. I can take a shower, I can do my laundry, and get up and go to work.

I'm certified as a cook right now. I got all the credentials. There's nothing I can't cook. You leave me alone, I can cook it. In a way I miss it because it gives me a peace of mind that I can create something. I can take something from nothing and make a meal out of it.

Recently I had two heart attacks, so I went to work as a security guard. Where they got me at right now I don't care too much for, because it's underneath a viaduct. These last few weeks, it was really cold underneath there.

I checked with my heart doctor yesterday. He said as long

as you don't have any stress, you'll be all right. Like to-night [at a church service] when they said "peace," I was like, "Yeah, I got the patent on it." I can't afford to get stressful or out of sequence. 'Cause the doctor said the next one might kill me.

Sometimes I might hear a person say something like "Man, I slapped that dude upside his head the other day," and I was like, "Man, I used to do that." Or "I slapped my old lady a couple of times." Man, I used to do that. And then I sit back and realize, "What did I do that for?"

I got a little grandbaby. That's my pride and joy. He calls me Paw Paw. He's a year and a half old now. When he comes over and visits me, he's like my own. He's always comical. You know how they are when they're babies; they're always comical. He won't sleep with his mother, he won't sleep with his father, when he's around me. He won't listen to nothing they say when he's around me. I guess I spoiled him.

I make sure I leave my house around 4:30, 5 o'clock, every Tuesday when I'm not working, and just come up here and see what's going on. I've always been the type of guy that'll come to a place early. If I'm going to go, I'm going to be there on time or early. 'Cause I just wanna see what's going on. Just for the company.

I'd like to find me a nice wife. I'd even get married to a woman that's got kids. I feel kind of lonely on Christmas Day. You ain't got nobody to open up the package with or say "Merry Christmas." You know.

During the week, I don't go nowhere. I don't have that many friends or many associates. That's the way I like it. I figure if you have too many friends or too many associates, they start nagging you and getting in your business.

I don't even know who my next-door neighbor is. I don't even know who lives across the hall from me. I come in, I go to my room, turn my TV on. I'll have my diet Coke and sit there and drink it and watch TV till I fall asleep. Then I'll get up and take my shower and get ready to go to work.

I love sports. I like to watch hockey. I like to watch football. I don't care too much for baseball. I like wrassling. I like boxing. I watch all the old westerns, like old John Wayne movies, *Bonanza*, stuff like that. I love *Perry Mason*. Matter of fact, *Perry Mason* comes on tonight at 8 o'clock. After that is *The Untouchables* at 9 o'clock. And after that is *Sanford and Son*. And after that is *Andy Griffith*. I got the schedule down pretty well.

Right now I feel pretty good 'cause I got a job. I got money in my pocket. I ain't got the best living conditions in the world, but at least it's paid for. At least I got a place to lay my head at night. At least I can take a shower when I want to.

Lori G.

Lorraine

"GLORIA"

I met my kids' dad on the Clark bus. I was with my mother, and she told him he should smile more, or something like that. He turned around to see me—then he was smiling a lot more. The next day he showed up at the restaurant that was not too far from my house, where I was a waitress, and introduced himself. We're still good friends. Even though the marriage didn't work out, we're not enemies or nothing like that.

My daughter, she's 21. She's working two jobs, so I see her whenever she can, but not too much. My son, he's living in Iowa. He's 25. He's always been shy and nervous, and he has a stuttering problem and slight learning disability. He's a good man, though. I tell him he's very handsome and he will find somebody, but these things take time.

There are some parents that give their kids what they want because they have a good type of income, and then there are some parents that don't have too good of an income, and you have to make every cent count. It would be nicer to have been one of them parents that could just say, "Okay, I'll give you this, I'll give you this."

Now I have a fiancé. We've been together 12 years. When I met him, I was going through a second divorce. The man that I was married to was a police officer. He used to beat me up all the time, even for being five or 10 minutes late. I thought for a while that it was going to be like that for the rest of my life. When we finally divorced and I met my fiancé, I was a wreck. He helped me through everything, and that was more than I could ever have asked for.

We stay with his brother, 'cause his brother owns the house, and everybody gets along. Usually before my fiancé comes home from work, he'll bring me a cup of coffee from McDonald's. He appreciates that I do a lot around the house, because him and his brother, they don't know how to clean house too well. The last time I went to see my son in Iowa, they were trying to wash clothes, and they broke the machine. It was a Maytag. I couldn't believe it.

I've always enjoyed coming here, and I always find peace of mind during the service. The doors are open; it's like friends here, friends there. That makes me happy. See, I live in Park Ridge, and the neighbors aren't really too friendly because they're more . . . upper. Which is fine. But when I come here, I don't have to deal with that.

I'm hoping and praying that me and my fiancée do get married eventually, 'cause he's been good to me. It's just not the right timing as far as finances.

"LUIS"

I was born in Puerto Rico, but my mother was Dominican. I've been in Chicago since I was two. We grew up on the West Side of Chicago, which is now the black West Side. But there used to be a scattering of Latinos there.

My parents got divorced when I was about 11 years old. It broke my heart, 'cause I love my daddy. He was a strict disciplinarian—he was God. And I missed him terribly.

In 1965 we moved up to Logan Square. I was going to Malcolm X College, found myself partying too much, and decided to get a job with the phone company. I was only going to take it for a year and go back to school. The money got too good. Lo and behold, I stayed 27 years.

My worst winter as a telephone man, it was -77°F wind chill factor and I had to spend four hours on a pole. I cursed my parents for bringing me from Puerto Rico to Chicago to die on a pole.

I made a decent buck, and I was able to eventually get married and raise this lady's two kids and buy a house. She had two children from a white guy, but I raised the kids like they were mine. That's the finest, hardest work I ever did. I'm proud of them, and I love them like they were mine, and they love me. I haven't seen them in 10 years. I got two grandbabies I've never seen. That's part of life.

When I was married, I got busted for drinking on the job, and I went to a little drug treatment center. I relapsed, and my wife kicked me right out the very same day. She called me a worthless piece of shit, not worth the life that God gave me.

I became homeless and wound up in Uptown. I was 50 years old, and I was completely alone for the first time in my life. I knocked on every door, trying to get some kind of help. I would go to Lawrence and Marine Drive by this water fountain and a big tree, and I would cry. I was in despair of my life.

I remembered something my brother had told me. He said, "You know, it's only when you are brokenhearted and contrite, when we done beat all the pride out of you, that's when God wants to hear from you, because that's when you're your most honest."

So I said the Sinner's Prayer. I said, "Lord, you see me here. I'm homeless. I'm old. I believe I'm killing my father of a broken heart. And if I kill my father of a broken heart, I don't deserve anything in this life or the next life, because my daddy don't deserve that." I said, "Lord, save me. In the name of Jesus, save me." One week later, a bed opened up for me in the drug program.

Now I gave that glory to Jesus. You gotta have God in your life, and a little hope and faith, and you can improve your situation.

I remember being a telephone man, I had obstacles every day that I had to overcome. In an hour, your boss is going to want you to finish this job. There can't be nothing about, "Oh, this is too hard." No, no, you overcome these things. That's what obstacles do. They make you strong.

I have a little rhythm. I used to play saxophone in a high school band. When I started going to college, these guys switched me over to conga drums, and I've been on them ever since. In Chicago I'm known, because I play with a lot of African dance troupes. It's a hard career to make money off of, you know. But it's a calling that just makes you keep coming back. The musical talent, it keeps you out of trouble.

My father's now 85 years old, and he looks better than I do. He's got a $375,000 home in Tinley Park. His wife is a registered nurse, and they go somewhere in the world for two weeks every year. That's the highlight of my week, seeing my daddy. I love him so much. It's beautiful.

I have one sister. We look so much alike. I call her every time I put some money on my phone. I'm dying to see her, man. I can't leave the county of Cook 'cause I'm on probation. I wrote this check for this guy, and he turned out to have stolen the check from a little old lady's car. I said, "Hey, I'm not a criminal, I'm a Christian." They said, "Well, you look like you a criminal to me. Is that or is that not that little old lady's checkbook? Is that or is that not your signature?" I was just coming home from the Salvation Army, man. I was going to go *watch* Judge Judy. I didn't know I was going to be in *front of* Judge Judy.

I started coming here [to RCS] about a year ago. I like the way you have these ladies around that kind of hostess you. That just makes you feel more human. When you're homeless, you're most of the time by yourself, in your own thoughts. That's too much in your head. You go crazy and you don't even know that you're crazy. But you have a nice pretty lady sitting by you talking all night, it reminds you that you're a worthwhile human being.

Now my thoughts are clearer. I don't do no hanging out in the streets no more. I know what I need to stay away from, and I stay away from it, and I keep my nose in the Bible and the Holy Koran. And God looks out for me. I'm truthful to him. I don't lie to him. I don't play with him. And so my life is improving, slowly. Thank you, thank you, Father. Thank you so much.

I need religion in my life. I need the company of people, you know? But good people. No riff-raff, thieves, lying people. I just need somewhere I can die with grace. And a sanctuary.

I'm doing all right. I'm doing all right. I'm working on getting a license, and I'm gonna get myself a little car. I'm on disability, and I just got a notice from Rod Blagojevich saying I can get those free rides. That's nice. That's great. That's wonderful. It's a wonderful life. It's what you make it, you know?

ACKNOWLEDGMENTS

I'm grateful beyond words to everyone who agreed to be interviewed for *A Friend That I Can Do For*. Abiding thanks for many reasons to Charlie Simokaitis, Madison Berry, Lori Gee, Kevin Goodman, Fran Holiday, Andrea Knepper, Claudia Montgomery, Nate Parkes, Bonnie Perry, Allison Schloss, Beth Taylor, and Wendy Vasquez, and to my dear husband, David Figlio.

—Anne Ford

It was a powerful and humbling year of Tuesday nights. Thanks to everyone for the opportunity to make photographs with you.

—Charlie Simokaitis

CPSIA information can be obtained at www.ICGtesting.com
Printed in the USA
LVOW08s0958150114

369512LV00004B/9/P